F

Alexander Kennedy

Amazon.com/author/alexanderkennedy

Contents

Prologue

"Fifty million Frenchmen can't be wrong."—
popular saying.

The French were mad for Benjamin Franklin.
The world had never seen anything like it.
Heroes of later centuries, like Charles
Lindbergh or Neil Armstrong, would get a
taste of what Franklin experienced in those
years, but in his time, public celebrity—as
opposed to the reverence for kings or other
nobility—was still a new phenomenon. Public
opinion was only just discovering its own
strength; indeed, before the 1770s, few people
would have even acknowledged that there was
such a thing as "public opinion." In his
celebrity, as in so many other things, Franklin
was a pioneer.

He had been sent by the new American
government in December 1776, only a few
months after he had served on the committee
that had drafted the Declaration of

Independence (see Chapter 5). Thomas Jefferson had done almost all of the writing, of course, but Franklin had contributed here and there, including one of the document's best-known phrases; where Jefferson had written "we hold these truths to be sacred and undeniable," Franklin had revised the sentence to the famous "we hold these truths to be self-evident." And then he was off, crossing the ocean for France.

It's no exaggeration to say that the whole revolution hinged on Franklin's mission. The British military was the world's most formidable war machine. In the course of the Revolutionary War, the British army would at some point take and hold every American city. George Washington had wisely abandoned his dreams of a set-piece battle in which he annihilated the British forces, and instead was concentrating on simply holding his army together until the British government gave up on the war. But even if Washington could survive on land, the colonists were hopelessly outmatched at sea. Without French ships, the British could continue to shuttle their troops up and down the colonies with impunity.

Luckily for Franklin—and for America—his reputation preceded him. His groundbreaking work Experiments and Observations on Electricity had been translated into French in 1752 on the recommendation of the Comte de Buffon, the greatest naturalist of his day, and on the express order of King Louis XV; the king had also sent his personal compliments to the author. (For more on Franklin's experiments, see Chapter 6.) After exchanging letters with many French admirers, Franklin visited in person in 1767 and 1769, each time making a celebrated appearance at court. He joked in his letters that he was becoming so French that "I was once very near making love to my friend's wife"—though in reality he never had more than a middling grasp on the language.

The France of Franklin's day was deep in the grip of a cult of simplicity, best exemplified by the works of Jean-Jacques Rousseau. "Man is born free, and everywhere he is in chains," Rousseau wrote, lamenting the corrupting influence of human society. To these aristocrats, the newborn United States seemed like a fresh start, the simple, innocent country of Rousseau's dreams. By criticizing and satirizing the aristocracy of which they themselves were a part, these French elites were acting much like a cartoon character who saws off the branch on which he himself is sitting. They believed they could play at despising the nobility without actually giving up its privileges, and many of them would pay for this folly with their heads.

But in 1776, France's own revolution was more than a decade in the future. Franklin, a political genius if ever there was one, saw immediately how this cult of innocence would benefit his cause, and took to donning a beaver fur cap for all his public appearances, even at court. He dressed in his simplest clothes, and stopped powdering his hair. He deliberately broke court etiquette when meeting with the new king, Louis XV's grandson Louis XVI, using simple, "republican" manners to interact with the king and his court rather than the established protocols. As historian Simon Scharma has written, Franklin had the vital gift of knowing "how to be impolite without being rude."

The French ate it up. They called him "The Electrical Ambassador," both for his scientific discoveries and his electrifying effects on the crowds. With every month, and every public appearance, Franklin's fame grew, and with it, the French devotion to the cause of American freedom. In the words of biographer Gordon S. Wood, "Franklin was the most potent weapon the United States possessed in its struggle with the greatest power on earth," and the British Prime Minister, Lord Rockingham, wrote that the government "trembled" at Franklin's mission.

Lord Rockingham was right to tremble. After American general Horatio Gates captured a large British force at the Battle of Saratoga in 1777, Franklin arranged a meeting with a British agent in Paris, letting it be understood that he intended to discuss peace terms. The ruse worked. Louis and his foreign minister, Vergennes, hurriedly agreed to start supporting the rebels. This aid was at first only a trickle, but Franklin spent the next four years opening it wider and wider. His diplomacy would pay its ultimate dividends at the Battle of Yorktown, when a French naval blockade allowed General George Washington to capture a massive British force under General Cornwallis.

Meanwhile, Franklin's popularity in France only continued to rise. There seemed to be no limits. One observer wrote, no doubt with some exaggeration, that every home in France now had a picture of Franklin above their mantel. Images of "Doctor Franklin" had become an industry unto themselves. There were prints, of course, but also Doctor Franklin inkwells, Doctor Franklin medallions, Doctor Franklin cotton wraps, Doctor Franklin vases, Doctor Franklin snuffboxes, Doctor Franklin porcelain, Doctor Franklin candies, Doctor Franklin clocks, Doctor Franklin handkerchiefs—the list goes on and on.

Gordon Wood suggests that Franklin may have surpassed everyone else in world history to that date, even monarchs, in the sheer proliferation of his likeness. Louis XVI, perhaps a touch jealous, presented one of Marie Antoinette's ladies-in-waiting, Diane de Polignac, with a chamberpot with Franklin's face painted inside as a joke. Franklin was the subject of more serious artists, too: Joseph-Siffred Duplessis, Jean-Baptiste Greuze, and J.F. de L'Hospital painted him, while Jean-Antoine Houdon and Jean-Jacques Caffiéri sculpted his bust. Franklin wrote to his daughter that the makers of French knick-knacks "have made your father's face as well-known as that of the moon."

The honors continued to roll in. Franklin was made the grandmaster of France's most prestigious Masonic lodge. (For more on Franklin's Masonic beliefs, see Chapter 4.) In April 1778, he found himself at the Academy of Science as that other great Enlightenment icon, François-Marie Arouet, better known by his pen name of Voltaire. Voltaire was an old man now, too, and in fact would die only a month later. But that night he was still out and about, and he and Franklin embraced before a roaring crowd. When the crowd demanded still more, Franklin kissed his French counterpart on both cheeks. The audience went wild.

Poor Richard's Almanack was translated into French that year, and became the best-selling book in Paris. Crowds watched for Franklin outside his home, and soon he could no longer set foot out of doors without the French public thronging around him. A number of these were French noblemen, or pretended noblemen, seeking commissions to join Washington's army in pursuit of liberty and glory. Franklin proved himself as good a talent scout as he was at almost everything else, politely rebuffing the most delusional while passing along two future heroes of Washington's staff, the Marquis de Lafayette and the Prussian Baron von Steuben, with hearty recommendations.

One of Louis XVI's ministers, the economist Anne Robert Jacques Turgot, even coined a Latin motto for Franklin: Eripuit coelo fulmen, sceptrumque tyrannis. ("He snatched lightning from the heavens and the scepter from tyrants.") Soon this motto, too, was inscribed everywhere, and the iconography of Franklin and lightning became a commonplace symbol for liberty. In Jacques Louis David's painting of the Tennis Court Oath—an iconic moment of the French Revolution—a lightning bolt appears in the sky in a clear reference to Franklin, though he had long since returned to America.

Franklin made this return voyage in 1785, after eight full years in France and after having helped negotiate the Treaty of Paris that ended the war. It was the greatest triumph of a career full of them, an astonishing ascent for a boy who fifty years before had been a fugitive, on the run from his indentured apprenticeship. Since then, Franklin had made himself one of America's first great publishers, and though the world did not yet know it, he had also written America's first truly great book, his still-secret Autobiography. He had pioneered the scientific study of electricity, discovering and defining such basic terms as "battery," "charge," and "electrify." He had published seminal work on ocean currents that would one day cut the duration of transatlantic voyages by two full weeks. He had done more than any man save George Washington to achieve American independence. And amazingly, his best years were still not yet behind him—at the Constitutional Convention two years later, he would propose a Great Compromise that would make the Constitution itself possible.

How could one man accomplish so much in a single lifetime? The following pages will attempt to answer that question.

Introduction

"Early to bed and early to rise makes a man healthy, wealthy and wise." – **Benjamin Franklin**

Benjamin Franklin, one of the leading figures of early American history, was a great polymath. He was extraordinarily successful in a wide range of endeavors, and was known by many names and titles, each of which highlighted his diverse interests and accomplishments. Franklin was a statesman, author, printer, publisher, political theorist, scientist, inventor, civic activist, statesman, diplomat, postmaster, businessman, humorist, and celebrated free thinker. Franklin has been called "America's Renaissance Man," and was emblematic of the fledgling American nation's spirit.

Born into a Boston family of modest means, Franklin had little in the way of formal education. Despite this lack of schooling, he became a successful entrepreneur, managing an expansive printing business in Philadelphia, and he prospered. Franklin remained an active public figure for his entire life, especially in Philadelphia, where he started a lending library, hospital, and college, and where he was recognized for his electrical experiments, innovative inventions, and a wide range of scientific interests. He also served in the Second Continental Congress, provided significant input in the Declaration of Independence, and was a key figure during negotiations for the Treaty of Paris that concluded the American Revolution. His final significant act of public service came in 1787 when he served as a delegate to the convention that produced the Constitution of the United States of America.

As a scientist, Franklin is still regarded as a major figure in the American Enlightenment and the study of physics for his experiments, discoveries, and theories regarding electricity.

As an inventor, he is known for many conveniences and necessities, such as the lightning rod, bifocal glasses, and the Franklin stove, along with numerous other inventions and discoveries.

As a public servant, Franklin conceptualized and facilitated the foundation of many civic organizations, including Philadelphia's first fire department and an educational academy, which is now known as the University of Pennsylvania.

Chapter 1:
Early Life &
Viewpoints

Ancestry and Family

Benjamin Josiah Franklin was born in Boston on January 17th, 1706 to Josiah Franklin and Abiah Folger.

Josiah Franklin was an English-born businessman. Born in the village of Ecton, Northamptonshire on December 23rd, 1657, Josiah was the ninth and final child of his parents, Thomas and Jane Franklin.

An industrious young man, Josiah Franklin worked as a fabric dyer in Ecton, England. In 1677, he married his first wife, Anne Child. Over the next few years, the couple had three children together— Elizabeth, Samuel, and Hannah. In 1682, Josiah, his wife, and three children moved to Boston. Upon his arrival, Josiah found work as a tallow chandler and soap boiler, because his previous profession was not in demand at the time. In Boston, then known as the Massachusetts Bay Colony, he served as the tithingman of the Old South Church.

After the family moved to Boston, Josiah and Anne had four more children— Josiah Jr., Ann, Joseph (I), who died soon after birth, and Joseph (II), named for his deceased older brother. In July of 1689, Anne Child Franklin died from complications giving birth to her seventh child. Josiah, left alone to raise their seven children, took a second wife not long after Anne's death. In November of 1689, Josiah married a prominent colonial woman named Abiah Folger in the Old South Meeting House.

Abiah Folger was born on August 15th, 1667, in Nantucket, Massachusetts to Peter Foulger (the surname later spelled Folger by his descendants), a schoolmaster, miller, and surveyor, and Marry Morrill Foulger, a former indentured servant. Abiah's family were among those who fled to Massachusetts from England in 1635 to establish a purified Congregationalist Christianity when King Charles I of England began the persecution of Puritans.

Abiah Folger Franklin went on to bear ten children: John, Peter, Mary, James, Sarah, Ebenezer, Thomas, Benjamin, Lydia, and Jane. Josiah Franklin had a total of seventeen children with his two wives. Benjamin Josiah Franklin was born in Boston on January 17th, 1706. His father, Josiah Franklin, was fifty-one, and his mother was thirty-nine. Benjamin was Josiah's eighth child with Abiah Franklin; he was the fifteenth child in Josiah's large family, and the youngest of his ten sons.

Virtue, Religion, and Personal Beliefs

Franklin was born into a religious home and believed in God his entire life. His parents and grandparents were devout Puritans, and they attended the Old South Church, a Puritan congregation in Boston. While Puritans were not as stern and severe as many stereotypes indicate, they focused on piety and devotion to their faith. Franklin's parents wanted young Benjamin to become a minister, as it was a sign of honor for a family like theirs. In Puritan New England, ministers were among the most educated and respected members of society. In his autobiography, Franklin joked that he was his father's "tithe" to the church, meaning that he was the son expected to become a minister and bring honor to the entire family.

Franklin's father was heavily influenced by Puritan preacher Cotton Mather. He was a family friend, and a copy of his book, *Bonifacius: Essays to Do Good,* helped instill a strong sense of societal responsibility in Benjamin. This book preached voluntary associations that "do good" to benefit society as a whole. During his teenage years, Benjamin adopted the penname *Silence Dogood* as an homage to this book's influence on his life. The values he learned from this text combined with his natural resourcefulness and organizational skills made him a vital and influential force in the establishment of voluntarism as an enduring institution in American society.

Despite his parents' intention for him to join the church, Franklin was heavily influenced by the Enlightenment movement, and adopted Deism. In his autobiography, he described himself as a deist, although he insisted that he was still a Christian. He retained a strong faith in God, and believed it was a crucial source of righteousness in mankind and that it was a providential actor in history. He later pointed to it as a significant factor responsible for America's independence. Franklin embraced the idea that the new nation could survive only if the people who lived in it were virtuous.

Franklin often professed the belief that organized religion was required to keep men righteous, though he did not often attend services himself. When he stopped attending church, Franklin wrote in his autobiography:

"Sunday being my studying day, I never was without some religious principles. I never doubted, for instance, the existence of the Deity; that He made the world, and governed it by His providence; that the most acceptable service of God was the doing good to man;

that our souls are immortal; and that all crime will be punished, and virtue rewarded, either here or hereafter."

Franklin's religious background and his desire to encourage virtuous behavior and strong moral character became part of the American zeitgeist, and was a key factor in shaping the character of the nation.

Shortly before he died in 1790, Franklin wrote a letter to the president of Yale University, Ezra Stiles. In the letter, he explained some of his views on religion:

"As to Jesus of Nazareth, my Opinion of whom you particularly desire, I think the System of Morals and his Religion, as he left them to us, the best the world ever saw or is likely to see; but I apprehend it has received various corrupt changes, and I have, with most of the present Dissenters in England, some Doubts as to his divinity; tho' it is a question I

do not dogmatize upon, having never studied it, and I think it needless to busy myself with it now, when I expect soon an Opportunity of knowing the Truth with less Trouble. I see no harm, however, in its being believed, if that belief has the good consequence, as it probably has, of making his doctrines more respected and better observed; especially as I do not perceive that the Supreme takes it amiss, by distinguishing the unbelievers in his government of the world with any particular marks of his displeasure."

Franklin's Thirteen Virtues

When he was twenty years old, Franklin developed a set of thirteen virtues through which he sought to develop and improve his moral character. He planned to improve each of these virtues through a scientific and logical process and, as a result, achieve moral perfection. Franklin sought to cultivate these virtues, and his approach to self-improvement lasted throughout his life, and he continued to practice them until he died. In his autobiography, Franklin lists these thirteen virtues:

- **Temperance**. Eat not to dullness; drink not to elevation.

- **Silence**. Speak not but what may benefit others or yourself; avoid trifling conversation.

- **Order**. Let all your things have their places; let each part of your business have its time.

- **Resolution**. Resolve to perform what you ought; perform without fail what you resolve.

- **Frugality**. Make no expense but to do good to others or yourself; i.e., waste nothing.
- **Industry**. Lose no time; be always employ'd in something useful; cut off all unnecessary actions.

- **Sincerity**. Use no hurtful deceit; think innocently and justly, and, if you speak, speak accordingly.

- **Justice**. Wrong none by doing injuries, or omitting the benefits that are your duty.

- **Moderation**. Avoid extremes; forbear resenting injuries so much as you think they deserve.
- **Cleanliness**. Tolerate no uncleanliness in body, clothes, or habitation.

- **Tranquility**. Be not disturbed at trifles, or at accidents common or unavoidable.

- **Chastity**. Rarely use venery but for health or offspring, never to dullness, weakness, or the injury of your own or another's peace or reputation.

- **Humility**. Imitate Jesus and Socrates.

His original list included twelve virtues, but a Quaker friend of his suggested that Franklin was often considered proud and overbearing, especially in conversation. Franklin typically interrupted his conversational partners to stress his opinion of a point. In an effort to cure himself of this character flaw (and perhaps improve opinions of his demeanor), Franklin added Humility to his list. Franklin did not believe he met with much success in the reality of this virtue, but believed that he lived up to the appearance of it. He adjusted his language in such circumstances so as to prove himself more eager to hear the opinions of others. In the end, Franklin found that his conversations with others were more pleasant as a result.

Franklin did not attempt to work on all thirteen virtues at once. Instead, he worked on one each week, "leaving all others to their ordinary chance." He believed that mastery of one would lead to improvement of the next. Using a notebook with a chart, Franklin marked his progress each day and week, until he completed a full cycle of the thirteen virtues in thirteen weeks, totaling four cycles a year. Franklin compared his system to a gardener who, rather than attempting to pull out all of the weeds at once, instead worked to improve one garden bed at a time, completing work on one before moving to the second.

Franklin indicated in his autobiography that the virtue of Order was the most difficult for him, both with regard to his business affairs and handling his personal belongings. This observation is particularly revelatory, since in the rest of his life, Franklin's organizational skills worked most to his advantage, and because his system of improving these virtues was both logical and organized.

Franklin related an anecdote in which he brought an axe to a smith in order to have the entire surface of it ground until it all shone as brightly as the edge. The smith agreed to do it if Franklin turned the wheel while the smith pressed the broad side of the axe on the stone. Turning the wheel with such resistance was exhausting. After some time, the smith said the axe was speckled, and encouraged Franklin to continue turning until the axe was bright. Instead, Franklin decided that he now preferred a speckled axe best.

Franklin's anecdote illustrates the point that while Franklin had not achieved perfect character where Order was concerned, he had at least improved. He further states that having a perfect character might make his acquaintances jealous, and that "a benevolent man should allow a few faults in himself, to keep his friends in countenance."

While Franklin did not live completely by his virtues— and by his own admission fell short of them many times— he believed the attempt made him a better man, and that the effort contributed greatly to his success and happiness. In his autobiography, he devoted more pages to this plan than to any other single point, suggesting that this practice was greatly important to him. Franklin wrote, "Tho' I never arrived at the perfection I had been so ambitious of obtaining, but fell far short of it, yet I was, by the endeavor, a better and a happier man than I otherwise should have been if I had not attempted it."

Views on Slavery

Slavery was a common practice during Franklin's lifetime, and slaves in Philadelphia were numerous. In 1750, half of the landowners with established estates owned slaves, and fifteen percent of Philadelphia dock workers were slaves. It is unclear how many slaves he owned during his lifetime, but the number is as high as seven, two of whom worked for him in his home and businesses. Franklin participated in the practice of slavery in many typical ways. He allowed slaves to be sold in his business, he posted bills calling for the capture of runaway slaves, and he profited from international and domestic slave trading.

In later years, however, Franklin came to view slavery as a loathsome practice that contradicted the principles of the American Revolution. He became a "cautious abolitionist" and an outspoken critic of slavery. Franklin served as president of an abolitionist society in Pennsylvania in 1787, and presented a petition to Congress in 1790 urging it to grant liberty "to those unhappy men who alone in this land of freedom are degraded into perpetual bondage." The petition was ignored, but Franklin continued to support the cause for freedom until his death, and even included a stipulation in his will requiring his daughter and her husband to free their slave in order to receive their inheritance.

Franklin even attempted to open a school to educate Philadelphia's slaves in 1758, though it never came to fruition. When he returned from England in 1762, Franklin's dedication to the anti-slavery movement became even more fervent, and by as late as 1770, he had freed his own slaves. He advocated against slavery, and attempted to fight the system that allowed it, including the international slave trade. Despite his strong stance against it, however, Franklin did not publicly debate the issue when it was brought up at the Second Constitutional Convention in 1787. Ever the diplomat, Franklin managed to see both sides of the issue of slavery and never quite fully removed himself from its principles and practices. He realized that the unity of the new nation was fragile, and too strong a stance on abolition may result in disaster for the United States. So instead, he swallowed his beliefs, and attempted to put the nation before human rights.

Early Life in Boston

Benjamin had a strong relationship with his father, Josiah, who had a great influence on him. Josiah originally hoped for a life as a minister for Benjamin, but in a crowded household with thirteen children to feed, there was no room for luxury. Josiah could not afford to send his son to school for more than two years of formal education. Clergymen needed many years of formal schooling, so Josiah's hopes for his son to become a minister faded. Josiah insisted that each of his sons learn a trade, and so at age ten, Benjamin was put to work in his cash-strapped father's soap shop.

Benjamin hated the business of soap making. Dipping wax and cutting wicks did nothing to ignite young Benjamin's eager imagination and adventurous spirit, and he soon grew restless and unhappy. His father accommodated him, and took him to shops in Boston to see different artisans such as joiners, bricklayers, turners, and braziers at work, hoping he would find some trade attractive. None won his interest. Despite this, Franklin later noted in his autobiography that he found these experiences useful, and learned enough from them that he was able to do small jobs around his own home when a regular workman could not be had. Franklin later used his varied skills to build small machines for his experiments.

Benjamin learned to read at a young age, and loved it. As a child, what little money he earned for himself was spent on books of all kinds. It was this fondness for literature that eventually determined his career. His older brother, James, was a printer. He needed an apprentice, and so when Ben was twelve years old, James took him on with their father's blessing.

Apprenticeship in Boston

When Benjamin was fifteen, James began publication of *The New England Courant*, the first true newspaper in Boston at the time.

Although there were two other papers published in Boston prior to James's, they only reprinted news from abroad. James's paper carried news from the colonies, articles, opinion pieces written by him and his friends, advertisements, and ship schedules. The paper gained reputation in the city, and was in popular demand.

As the paper gained attention, James's friends visited frequently to discuss the success and contents of it. Ben listened in on many of their conversations. An avid reader and writer himself, Ben wanted to write for the paper, but knew that his brother would never allow it.

Convinced that his brother would not publish anything he wrote, Franklin adopted a pseudonym. He developed the fictional character of Mrs. Silence Dogood, a middle-aged widow. Ben wrote letters signed accordingly, and slipped them under the door of the print shop at night so that no one would know the true author. Mrs. Dogood wrote a series of fourteen imaginative and witty letters to *The New England Courant*, which became a popular topic of conversation around town.

Mrs. Dogood offered sound advice and stern criticism of life in Boston. In one of her letters, Mrs. Dogood proclaimed, "Without freedom of thought there can be no such thing as wisdom and no such thing as public liberty without freedom of speech." Neither James nor the *Courant's* readers knew of Benjamin's ruse. Eventually, after the fourteen letters were written and published, Ben confessed that he had written them. While James's friends thought Ben was quite precocious and funny, James scolded his brother and was very jealous of the attention paid to him.

One distinct benefit of Ben's apprenticeship to his brother was access to more and better books. He used his wages to purchase as many books as he could, and the acquaintance of bookseller apprentices allowed him the opportunity to occasionally borrow books from their shops, though he always took care to return them quickly and in perfect condition. In an effort to return the books quickly, Franklin often sat up reading long into the night. When he was around sixteen years of age, Franklin became ashamed of his lack of education and, proving himself industrious and scholarly once again, borrowed books and taught himself arithmetic, grammar, and philosophy.

James was a harsh employer, and he frequently mistreated and even beat his younger brother. In Franklin's autobiography, he describes their relationship as more of master and apprentice than brothers. James expected Franklin to perform any and all duties of an apprentice, and perhaps even more than would usually be expected, particularly from an apprentice who is also a relative, and who might reasonably expect a bit of indulgence or lenience. Franklin and James argued frequently, and often brought their disputes to their father who, according to Franklin, often sided with Benjamin. Frustrated with the harsh treatment and frequent beatings, and finding apprenticeship a tedious circumstance, Franklin wished for a way out. But despite the unhappy conditions of his apprenticeship, Ben learned much about newspaper work and publishing under his brother's harsh tutelage, and he was eventually able to put that knowledge to good use.

From an early age, Ben was an advocate of free speech. In 1722, James was jailed for three weeks for publishing material of a political nature in the *Courant* that was unflattering to the local governor. James and Franklin were both questioned, but Franklin was dismissed, as he was just an apprentice. In his autobiography, Franklin indicated that he does not recall the precise circumstances of James's accusation.

Other sources suggest the Franklins disagreed with members of Boston's powerful Puritan preaching family, the Mathers. Smallpox was a deadly disease at the time, and the Mathers supported inoculation; the Franklins believed inoculation made people sicker. While most Bostonians agreed with the Franklins' argument, they disapproved of the way James criticized the clergy during the public debate, and James was ultimately jailed for his views. In his autobiography, Franklin later conceded that, after losing one of his sons to smallpox, he regretted his stance on inoculation, and suggested that parents should consider this a safer option to avoid losing a child and experiencing regret as he had.

Despite their ongoing differences, Franklin took great offense at James's censure and imprisonment. During his brother's absence, Franklin managed the paper, and took the opportunity to make some negative remarks toward the governing body, which James seemed to appreciate. Others, however, began to see Franklin as something of a troublemaker with a gift for libel and satire. As part of James's penalty upon his discharge, an order from the House was issued, stating that "James Franklin should no longer print the paper called the '*New England Courant*.'"

There was no mention of whether another party was allowed to continue publishing the *Courant*, however, and after consultation with James's friends, it was decided that Benjamin would print the paper under his name instead. Because he was an apprentice, however, there was significant danger that this activity may result in James's further censure.

To avoid any potential legal trouble, Franklin's original indenture papers were returned to him with a full discharge written on the back, to be presented upon request. To ensure that Franklin would continue to be in James' service, however, new terms of indenture were drawn up for the remainder of his original term, and these papers were kept private. It was under these new terms that the publication of the *Courant* continued in Benjamin Franklin's name for several months.

After his release from jail, James was not particularly grateful to Ben for keeping the paper going, though he appreciated his brother's continued digs at the colonial government. He continued to harass and beat his brother from time to time, and eventually new arguments arose between them. Tired of his brother's continued harsh and tyrannical behavior, Franklin decided to leave his servitude to his brother once and for all. Even though he had three years remaining on his legally binding indentured service, Franklin counted on the fact that James would not opt to produce the new indenture papers to force him to stay. In his autobiography, Franklin admits that perhaps he took advantage of the circumstances, and conceded that though his brother was terribly harsh and had beaten him, it was possible that Franklin was, in his words, "too saucy and provoking."

Unable to find work in Boston, perhaps due to his brother's influence with other merchants and tradesmen, and having made himself unpopular with the local government, Franklin decided to move to New York to find work with a printer there. His father was firmly against the plan, however, and sided with James. Against his family's wishes, Franklin secretly fled Boston in 1723, escaping to New York before settling in Philadelphia,

which was his home base for the rest of his
life.

Chapter 2:
A New Life in Philadelphia

Escape to Philadelphia

Seventeen year old Franklin sold some of his books to raise enough money to leave, and a friend helped him book passage secretly on a ship bound for New York. He arrived three days later, with no money, no employment prospects, and no connections to help him along. He sought out the only printer in town, Mr. William Bradford, but he could offer Franklin no work. Instead, he referred him to his son in Philadelphia, whom he believed might be willing to hire an assistant.

Franklin set out on a boat bound for Amboy, leaving his few possessions behind to follow him by sea. The second evening of the journey, Franklin found himself feverish. He recalled having read somewhere that drinking large amounts of cold water might relieve a fever, and so he followed that prescription, "sweat plentifully most of the night," and found himself without fever in the morning. This is perhaps the first documented case of Franklin using direct knowledge from books to improve his life, something that he became quite talented at later. When he disembarked, Franklin continued his journey for fifty miles on foot to Burlington, where he was told he could find passage to take him the rest of the way to Philadelphia.

Franklin walked most of the day in the rain, and eventually arrived at an inn, soaked and tired. By this point in the journey, Franklin had begun to wish he had never left Boston. Exhausted, dirty, and hungry, he presented a rather dismal image as a traveler. He realized, based on the questions people asked, that he was suspected to be a runaway servant, and as such was in danger of being arrested. He managed to continue on his way without incident, and arrived the next evening just outside of Burlington at an inn kept by a man named Dr. Brown, with whom he struck up conversation. Dr. Brown realized that Franklin was well-read, and the two began a friendship that continued for many years.

The next morning, a Saturday, Franklin discovered that the boat he was supposed to board had already departed, and that no more were expected for several days. He found lodging with an old woman in town who was happy to host him until he found passage to Philadelphia. Walking by the river, Franklin met up with several people taking a boat on to Philadelphia. They accepted Franklin on board and, as Franklin later related, rowed all the way from Burlington to Philadelphia, where he arrived Sunday morning. And so, on a chilly Sunday morning in October, 1723, a tired and hungry Franklin landed at the Market Street wharf in Philadelphia and immediately set out to find food, work, and adventure.

Arrival in Philadelphia

In his autobiography, Franklin describes his first days in Philadelphia with a bit of poignancy and humor. The events he relates in the text provide insight into his character at this pivotal period of his life, but they also illustrate the dramatic progression he made from his early years, a young man with no money, no job, and no prospects, to a prominent and successful public figure.

Franklin describes his attire upon his arrival as his "working-dress," since his best clothes had still not arrived by sea. He was dirty from his long journey, but had spare shirts and stockings stuffed into his pockets. Fatigued and hungry from his travels, Franklin needed to find a place to rest and eat, but his funds were limited to a single Dutch dollar and one shilling in copper, which he gave to the people who owned the boat in exchange for his passage. Franklin stated that the boat owners refused his money since he helped with the rowing, but Franklin insisted that they take it, saying that a man is "sometimes more generous when he has but a little money than when he has plenty, perhaps thro' fear of being thought to have but little." Franklin understood that his appearance provided a poor first impression, and his wounded pride made him concerned that people considered him a pauper based on his presentation.

As Franklin travelled through Philadelphia, he found a bakery, and after some brief haggling and conversation, Franklin left with three large rolls of bread. With no room in his pockets, Franklin carried one roll under each arm and the third in his mouth. As he walked up Market Street, he passed the door of a man named Mr. Read, who eventually became his father-in-law. Inside the house, his future wife stood, likely noting his most ridiculous appearance. In his autobiography, Franklin, understanding his ridiculous appearance, looked back on the situation with good humor.

As he continued through the streets of Philadelphia, Franklin happened upon a woman and her child in need of food. Despite the fact that he had no more than the bread he had just purchased, Franklin gave them his two remaining rolls without question or hesitation, stating that he had no need because he had already had his fill from one. Rather than thinking forward to his next meal, Franklin saw the immediate need of the woman and her child and volunteered his aid. Franklin's outwardly focused personality and generous nature was demonstrated by this charitable act, as he had just given away what little he had rather than looking ahead to his future situation.

Finally, Franklin followed a group of well-dressed people who were all heading in the same direction. Always curious and interested, Franklin followed them to see where they were going, and ended up in a Quaker meeting house. Unafraid and confident, Franklin sat among them and, hearing nothing said (for Quaker meetings were and still are often silent prayer), promptly fell asleep until the meeting ended and someone woke him up. Franklin later stated that this was the first "house" in which he slept upon his arrival in Philadelphia.

Franklin asked a young Quaker man where he could find a place to stay, and was shown to a place called the Crooked Billet. As he ate his meal, Franklin's appearance again raised suspicion that he was a runaway. After eating, Franklin was shown to a room where he slept until six o'clock that evening, when he was called to supper. After he finished *that* meal, he then returned to bed and slept soundly until morning. In the morning he cleaned himself up to present as positive an impression as possible, and set off to see William Bradford's son, Andrew, about finding work.

Early Days in Philadelphia

As it turned out, Bradford did not have work to offer, but Franklin found employment with another printer, Samuel Keimer, who was just starting his business. Keimer found Franklin lodging at the home of John Read, where he met and then courted his landlord's daughter, Deborah. His trunk and clothing had finally arrived by then, and Franklin said he made a much more respectable appearance in Deborah's eyes than their first meeting when she saw him walking down the street with a roll stuck in his mouth.

In 1723, seventeen-year-old Franklin proposed to Deborah Read, who was fifteen. Read's mother, however, was wary of allowing her young daughter to marry Franklin. Benjamin was on his way to London at Governor Sir William Keith's request, and had not yet achieved what she thought was an acceptable level of financial stability. Recently widowed herself, Mrs. Read did not give her blessing to the marriage.

Franklin's work as a printer had gained him the notice of Sir William Keith, the British governor of Pennsylvania, who pledged his aid to help him start his own business. The conditions of their agreement required Franklin to go to London first to buy a printing press. Franklin left for London in 1724 to purchase supplies from stationers, booksellers, and printers. The Governor promised to send a letter of credit to London, but did not follow through. When Franklin arrived in England, he found that Keith's letters of introduction never arrived as promised, and Franklin was obliged to remain in London for nearly two years to work in order to earn his fare home.

While in London, Franklin worked as a typesetter in a printer's shop in what is now the Church of St. Bartholomew the Great in the Smithfield area. During his stay, Franklin took full advantage of the city's cultural pleasures, and he regularly attended theater performances, spoke with patrons in coffee houses, and continued to indulge his lifelong passion for reading. Franklin, also a self-taught swimmer who had crafted his own wooden flippers, enjoyed many long-distance swims on the Thames River. He was finally able to return to Philadelphia in 1726 with the help of Thomas Denham, a merchant for whom Franklin worked as clerk, shopkeeper, and bookkeeper.

Marriage to Deborah Read

Franklin returned to Philadelphia in 1726 to find that Deborah Read had married while he was in London. However, she had been abandoned by her husband just a few months after the wedding. Shortly after their marriage, John Rodgers avoided his outstanding debts and prosecution by fleeing to Barbados with Deborah's dowry, leaving her behind. Because Rodgers's fate was unknown and he could not be confirmed to be dead, bigamy laws prevented Read and Franklin from marrying.

Despite this, they lived together, and Franklin established a common-law marriage with Deborah Read on September 1st, 1730. This also marks the point at which Franklin acknowledged an illegitimate son, William, and they took him into their home.

William Franklin was born in Philadelphia, Pennsylvania, but his mother's identity remains unknown to this day. The confusion regarding the details of William's birth and parentage exists because Ben Franklin was secretive about his son's origin, and he even told his own mother in 1750 that William was nineteen years old. Despite this confusion, William always referred to Deborah as his mother. There has been speculation that Deborah Read actually *was* William's mother, but because of his parents' common-law status, the circumstances of his birth were obscured to avoid political harm to Ben or to their marital arrangement.

In addition to William, Deborah and Franklin had two children together. Francis Folger Franklin was born in October of 1732, and sadly died of smallpox in 1736. Sarah Franklin was born in 1743. She went on to marry Richard Bache, with whom she had seven children, and she later cared for her father in his old age.

The Franklin family lived in Philadelphia throughout Franklin's life and career. Deborah's fear of the sea prevented her from accompanying Franklin on any of his extended trips to Europe, despite his repeated requests. In November of 1769, she wrote to him saying she was ill due to "dissatisfied distress" over his prolonged absence, but he did not return until his business at the time was finished.

Deborah Read Franklin died of a stroke in 1774, while Franklin was on an extended mission to England. He was unable to return until 1775.

Chapter 3:
The Prolific Publisher

Liberty and Necessity, Pleasure and Pain

In 1725, while still in London, Franklin published the first of many pamphlets, *A Dissertation Upon Liberty and Necessity, Pleasure and Pain.* The piece attacked conservative religion, which argued that humans lack free will and are therefore not morally responsible for their actions. In later years, Franklin renounced his original claims and burned all but one copy of the pamphlet, which he still held in his possession.

Over the next several years, Franklin held various jobs, such as bookkeeper, shopkeeper, and currency cutter. He returned to his familiar printing trade in 1728 when he printed paper money in New Jersey. Later that year, he and a fellow printer from Keimer's shop, Hugh Meredith, left Keimer's and opened their own printing and stationery shop, funded by Meredith's father. In early 1730, Franklin and Meredith were elected official government printers by the Pennsylvania Assembly, and later that year Franklin purchased Meredith's side of the business, becoming the sole proprietor at the age of twenty-four.

Necessity of a Paper Currency

In 1729, Franklin anonymously authored and published another pamphlet titled *The Nature and Necessity of a Paper Currency*, which brought public attention to the need for an increase in the paper money supply in Pennsylvania to stimulate the economy. As a result, Franklin successfully landed a contract to print paper money.

Franklin wrote that it was "a very profitable job, and a great help to me. Small favors were thankfully received. And, I took care not only to be in reality industrious and frugal, but to avoid all appearances to the contrary. I drest plainly; I was seen at no places of idle diversion. And, to show that I was not above my business, I sometimes brought home the paper I purchased at the stores thru the streets on a wheelbarrow."

With the money Franklin earned from his money-related employment, he was able to purchase the *Pennsylvania Gazette* newspaper from his former boss, Keimer.

Franklin the Newspaper Man

Franklin's old boss, Samuel Keimer, had started a newspaper in Philadelphia titled *The Universal Instructor in All Arts and Sciences and Pennsylvania Gazette.* After Samuel Keimer declared bankruptcy, Franklin took over the newspaper with its ninety subscribers. The

"Universal Instructor" feature of the paper consisted of a weekly page called "Chambers' Encyclopedia." Franklin eliminated this feature, dropped the majority of the long name, and the *Pennsylvania Gazette* was born.

The *Gazette* printed local news, excerpts from the London newspaper the *Spectator*, jokes, verses, humorous attacks against his publishing rival, Bradford, moral essays written by Franklin, elaborate hoaxes, and political satire. Franklin not only printed the paper, but often contributed pieces to the paper under aliases, either to emphasize points or to ridicule some fictitious yet typical reader. In Franklin's capable hands, the struggling publication was transformed into the most widely read paper in the colonies, and became one of the first to actually turn a profit. Among other firsts, the *Gazette* printed the first political cartoon, authored by

Franklin himself. It was later renamed *The Saturday Evening Post.*

Poor Richard's Almanac

Franklin's success grew, particularly with the publication of *Poor Richard's Almanac* in 1732. Franklin published the *Almanac* under the name of Richard Saunders, on which much of his popular reputation is based, using both original and borrowed content. It was no secret that Franklin was the true author, but his Saunders character repeatedly denied this fact. In addition to weather forecasts, astronomical information, and poetry, the *Almanac* included the wise and witty sayings of Richard Saunders, the publisher, and Bridget, his wife. Bridget Saunders was yet another pseudonym in Franklin's growing list.

Familiar sayings such as "Early to bed and early to rise, makes a man healthy, wealthy, and wise," "A penny saved is twopence dear," (often misquoted as "a penny saved is a penny earned"), and "Fish and visitors stink in three days" were part of the regular fare in the *Almanac*, which Franklin published for twenty-five consecutive years. The *Almanac* sold about ten thousand copies per year, which was a massive success at the time. Later, the most popular and remarkable sayings were collected and published in a standalone book.

Magazines did not exist in the colonies in any modern sense. The "magazines" of the time were mainly collections of reprints of stories and essays published abroad weeks or even months before. Benjamin Franklin started one of the first modern magazines in America. In 1741, Franklin began publishing *The General Magazine and Historical Chronicle for all the British Plantations in America*, the first original-content monthly magazine published in America. As the title suggests, the focus of the publication was on American interests rather than British ones.

In 1758, the same year he ceased publication of the *Almanac*, Franklin printed a sermon under yet another pseudonym, Father Abraham, an essay based on the concepts of work ethic and frugality titled *The Way to Wealth*. The text is a collection of adages and advice as presented in *Poor Richard's Almanac* and organized into a speech given by Father Abraham. Many of the sayings Father Abraham used in the essay continue to be familiar today, such as, "There are no gains without pains."

The Autobiography

Franklin's autobiography was not published while Franklin was alive. The first edition appeared in 1791 in French, not English, under the title *Mémoires de la vie privée de Benjamin Franklin*, and was released in Paris. This translation, which consisted only of the first part of Franklin's text, was based on a flawed transcript of Franklin's manuscript before he had revised it.

Franklin's autobiography was written as a sort of volume of moral instruction for his son. Franklin wrote the first eighty pages in 1771, when he was sixty-five years old, then set the work aside for nearly thirteen years. He returned to the work in 1784, when he was seventy-eight years old. He began work on Part Two, but completed only about seventeen pages before putting the work aside again for yet another four years. It wasn't until 1788, when Franklin was eighty-three years old and in failing health that he finally continued writing what he called his "Memoirs," finishing more than a hundred pages before his death at the age of eighty-four. According to outlines made by Franklin, the work was still largely unfinished.

The autobiography consists of four parts. The first three parts were initially published together in English in 1818 by Franklin's grandson, William Temple Franklin, in London. In this edition, Part Four was omitted, and his grandson took unauthorized stylistic liberties with the text. William Temple Franklin's version remained the standard edition of the autobiography for half a century, until John Bigelow purchased the original manuscript in France, and in 1868 published the most reliable text that had yet appeared.

Several editions appeared thereafter until 1981, when J.A. Leo Lemay and P.M. Zall published *The Autobiography of Benjamin Franklin: A Genetic Text*. This version attempted to show and include all revisions and cancellations from the original manuscript. This remains the most accurate edition of Franklin's autobiography.

Shop and Home Life

In addition to his printing business, Franklin also kept a shop where he sold a wide variety of goods, including legal blanks, ink, pens, paper, books, maps, pictures, chocolate, coffee, cheese, codfish, soap, linseed oil, broadcloth, tea, spectacles, lottery tickets, and stoves.

Before her death, Deborah assisted Franklin in the business, folding and binding pamphlets, maintaining the shop, and various other tasks. In his autobiography, Franklin says he was lucky to have a wife as "disposed to industry and frugality" as himself. He wrote: "We kept no idle servants, our table was plain and simple, our furniture of the cheapest. For instance, my breakfast was a long time bread and milk (no tea), and I ate it out of a twopenny earthen porringer with a pewter spoon."

As a result of this simple and frugal lifestyle, Franklin's wealth increased rapidly. "I experienced too," he wrote, "the truth of the observation, that after getting the first hundred pound, it is more easy to get the second, money itself being of a prolific nature."

By the relatively young age of forty-two, Franklin was able to retire from active business, and devoted his time and energy to his philosophical and scientific interests.

Chapter 4:
A Dedicated Public Servant

The Library Company

Franklin continued his civic contributions during the 1730s and 1740s. Among his chief accomplishments of this era was the launch of the Library Company in 1731. The ability to make friends was one of Benjamin Franklin's greatest traits, and the number of his acquaintances grew rapidly no matter where his travels took him. "I grew convinced," he wrote, "that truth, sincerity, and integrity in dealings between man and man were of the utmost importance to the felicity of life." Shortly after Franklin returned from London in the fall of 1727, the twenty-one year-old Franklin formed a literary, social, and self-improvement group for young men that met every Friday to debate morality, philosophy, and politics, and to discuss and critique the writings of its members. He called it the Junto.

Of this group, Franklin wrote:

"...I had formed most of my ingenious acquaintance into a club of mutual improvement, which we called the "Junto"; we met on Friday evenings. The rules that I drew up required that every member, in his turn, should produce one or more queries on any point of morals, politics, or natural philosophy, to be discussed by the company, and once in three months produce and read an essay of his own writing, on any subject he pleased. Our debates were to be under the direction of a president, and to be conducted in the sincere spirit of inquiry after truth, without fondness for dispute, or desire of victory; and, to prevent warmth, all expressions of positiveness in opinions, or direct contradiction, were after some time made contraband, and prohibited under small pecuniary penalties."

Its members were a group of "like minded aspiring artisans and tradesmen who hoped to improve themselves while they improved their community." Franklin modeled the Junto after the English coffeehouses that he frequented during his time in London, which were a key factor in spreading the ideas of the Enlightenment movement in Britain. He structured the group as a meeting to discuss current events and issues, and to offer solutions to the problems that faced the colonists. These meetings naturally progressed into the formation of many other Philadelphia organizations.

One of the discussed issues was the lack of a variety of reading material amongst the group, a direct result of the expense and scarcity of books at the time. Franklin proposed a solution:

"A proposition was made by me that since our books were often referr'd to in our disquisitions upon the inquiries, it might be convenient for us to have them altogether where we met, that upon occasion they might be consulted; and by thus clubbing our books to a common library, we should, while we lik'd to keep them together, have each of us the advantage of using the books of all the other members, which would be nearly as beneficial as if each owned the whole."

This sufficed for a while, but the members of the group soon wanted to expand their reading choices, and Franklin looked for a solution to the dilemma. He recognized that by pooling their resources, members of the group could afford to buy books from England, thus expanding their selection. From this realization was born the nation's first subscription library, The Library Company of Philadelphia, in 1731. Its charter was composed by Franklin in 1731, and in 1732, Franklin hired the first American librarian, Louis Timothee. The Library Company still exists, and is now a great scholarly and research library.

A Prominent Citizen

Franklin's contributions to Philadelphia life and society reached far beyond establishing the first circulating library in Philadelphia, which was one of the first in the country. Franklin's interest in public matters also extended to the paving and cleaning of city streets, better street lighting, and the organization of a police force and fire company.

Franklin held great influence with his fellow Philadelphia citizens, and he used this influence to develop many improvements for the general populace. Franklin was instrumental in the foundation of Pennsylvania Hospital, the first hospital in the colonies. Franklin and Dr. Thomas Bond obtained a charter from the state legislature to establish it, and he raised money to help fund the hospital in 1751. Franklin served on the hospital's original Board of Managers, as its first secretary, and as its second president. The hospital still stands today, and offers a unique blend of history and patient care, while serving as an enduring reminder of Franklin's legacy.

Fire Insurance and Prevention

Fire was a very dangerous threat to Philadelphians, and those who suffered fire damage to their homes often suffered irreversible economic loss. In 1752, Franklin helped found the Philadelphia Contribution for Insurance Against Loss by Fire, where citizens could purchase insurance in the event of such a catastrophe. Those with insurance policies were no longer destroyed financially in the event of a fire. The Contributionship is still in business today.

In addition to the insurance safeguard, Franklin wanted to raise public awareness about the city's need to improve its firefighting techniques. In a 1733 article in the *Pennsylvania Gazette*, Franklin described how fires were fought in Philadelphia: "Soon after it [a fire] is seen and cry'd out, the Place is crowded by active Men of different Ages, Professions and Titles who, as of one Mind and Rank, apply themselves with all Vigilance and Resolution, according to their Abilities, to the hard Work of conquering the increasing fire."

Franklin felt that goodwill and amateur firefighters were not sufficient, though, and he proposed a solution. In the February 4th issue in 1735 of the *Pennsylvania Gazette*, Franklin sent one of his anonymous letters to his own newspaper titled "Protection of Towns from Fire." Adopting the persona of an "old citizen," he admonished the current practices. Franklin insisted that chimney sweeps should only be allowed to operate if they were licensed by the city, and that they should also be held responsible for poorly performed work. He noted that Boston maintained "a club or society of active men belonging to each fire engine, whose business is to attend all fires with it whenever they happen." He concluded that, with regular practice and meeting, the skills of firefighters improved dramatically.

Urged by Franklin's persistence, a group of thirty men joined to form the Union Fire Company on December 7, 1736. Their equipment included leather buckets, which were to be brought to every fire. Homeowners were also required to keep leather fire-fighting buckets in their houses. The members met monthly to talk and learn about fire prevention and fire-fighting methods. His famous saying, "An ounce of prevention is worth a pound of cure," was actually fire-fighting advice. The end result of these efforts was a dramatic reduction in damage and fatalities caused by fires in Philadelphia.

American Philosophical Society

The American Philosophical Society owes its origin to Benjamin Franklin. It arose out of the Junto, and was formed by Franklin's official motion in 1743, though the organization dates its inception to the founding of the Junto, in 1727.

In Franklin's time, scientists were called philosophers. The American Philosophical Society offered members a scientific forum to exchange new ideas, including Franklin's electrical theories. From its inception, the society has boasted among its members many leading men in scientific fields from around the world.

The informal Junto gave way to a group of learned scientists. Early members concerned themselves with the study of what they believed were useful sciences. They wanted to improve farm and livestock production, and find ways to import new crops. They also wanted to make a better beer and find better ways to practice mapmaking, surveying, and charting. The early membership included naturalists, mathematicians, and "electricians" (a term that referred to those who experimented with electricity). Franklin soon grew disillusioned with the group, however, saying they were "very idle gentlemen."

Interest in the society fell off for a while, but as American resistance to British authority breathed new life into it. Younger APS members wanted to put their knowledge to use in order to prop up the colonial economy. One of the society's earliest important undertakings was the successful observation of the transit of Venus in 1769, which brought the group attention and recognition among European intellectuals.

Freemasons

Franklin's reputation grew quickly in Pennsylvania, and in 1731, he was initiated into the local Masonic Lodge. He quickly rose within the ranks of the Freemasons, and by 1734 was appointed the Grand Master of the Provincial Grand Lodge in Pennsylvania. That same year, he edited and published the first Masonic book in America, a reprint of James Anderson's Constitutions of the Free-Masons. Franklin was soon elected secretary of St. John's Lodge, and he held the position from 1735 until 1738. In March of 1752, Benjamin Franklin was part of a committee to establish the first Masonic building in the United States, a lodge in Philadelphia, Pennsylvania.

Franklin continued to be an active member of the fraternity, and was elected and appointed for many positions in the organization over the years. He remained a Freemason for the rest of his life.

Early Retirement

In 1747, Franklin retired from printing to pursue other endeavors. He created a partnership with his foreman, David Hall, the terms of which provided Franklin with a sizeable portion of the shop's profits. For eighteen years after his retirement, he received half of the profits from the shop. This lucrative business arrangement enabled Franklin to devote more leisure time to his studies and to conduct his scientific experiments. Within a few short years, he had made discoveries that earned him a reputation with educated persons throughout Europe, and especially in France.

In 1748, at the age of 42, Franklin had become one of the wealthiest and most successful men in Pennsylvania. He moved into a new house and acquired the first of his slaves to work in his home and businesses. Franklin's views on slavery evolved over many years of his life, ultimately bringing him to consider the entire institution of slavery inherently evil, resulting in him freeing his own slaves in the 1760s.

Just before he moved, Franklin published the pamphlet *Plain Truth,* which highlighted Pennsylvania's vulnerability to attack by the French and Native Americans. A volunteer militia was formed in response to his pamphlet, with funds raised by lottery, and Franklin was selected for the rank of Colonel for the regiment from Philadelphia.

Though Franklin was a soldier in the Pennsylvania militia at this time, he continued to be interested in electricity. His experiments and investigations into electrical phenomena were compiled in the 1751 publication *Experiments and Observations on Electricity.* Franklin conducted his famous kite-and-key experiment in 1752 in order to demonstrate that lighting was, in fact, electricity. He invented the lightning rod and coined new electricity-related terms such as "battery," "charge," "conductor," and "electrify," all of which are still part of our lexicon today.

Academy of Philadelphia

Franklin's tireless efforts at self-education earned him honorary degrees from Harvard, Yale, Oxford University, and the University of St. Andrews in Scotland. In 1749, Franklin wrote and published a pamphlet titled *Proposals Relating to the Education of Youth* and circulated it among some of Philadelphia's leading citizens. The pamphlet insisted that a college was necessary, and called upon any citizen who valued education to donate funds to build one. Franklin then did what he did best: he gathered a group of his friends and went to work to solve the problem. This resulted in the establishment of the Academy of Philadelphia, which still exists, though it has been renamed the University of Pennsylvania.

Franklin's associates in this endeavor included ten patriots who later signed the Declaration of Independence, and seven future signatories of the Constitution. He organized twenty-four trustees to form an institution of higher learning based on the proposals outlined in his essay. A building was purchased, and The Academy of Philadelphia opened its doors in 1751 on Philadelphia's Fourth Street. The school provided education to children of both the gentry and the working class. It was granted a charter in 1755, and graduated its first class of seven men on May 17th, 1757 with its first commencement ceremony. Franklin served as president of the school until 1755, and then as a trustee until his death in 1790. He helped create the original curriculum, which focused on the sciences, history, logic, mathematics, and geography. The college educated many future leaders of the United States, including twenty-one members of the Continental Congress and nine signers of the Declaration of Independence who were alumni of the school.

Public Life and Service

During the 1750s, Franklin took a more active interest in politics, and he was chosen to be an ambassador to England when tax disputes began. In 1757, he was appointed by the Pennsylvania Assembly to serve as the colony's agent in England. Accompanied by his son William, Franklin reached London in July of 1757, and from this point forward he spent a great deal of time traveling to and from Europe. Franklin sailed to London to represent Pennsylvania in negotiations over a long-standing dispute with the proprietors of the colony, the Penn family. He took William and his two slaves with him, but left Deborah and their daughter, Sarah, behind. He spent most of the next two decades in London, where he was drawn to the high society and intellectual salons of the cosmopolitan city.

After Franklin returned to Philadelphia in 1762, he traveled sixteen hundred miles touring the colonies to inspect the status of their postal systems. In 1764, through his political connections in the British government, he arranged for his son William to take office as New Jersey's royal governor. After Franklin lost his seat in the Pennsylvania Assembly in 1764, he was sent to England once again as the colony's agent to renew the petition for a royal government for Pennsylvania, which had not yet been granted.

He kept asking Deborah to come visit him in England. He wanted to remain there permanently, but she was terrified of nautical travel, and refused. Franklin made this trip to London without Deborah, who remained in Philadelphia. This was the last time the couple saw each other. Franklin did not return home before Deborah died of a stroke in 1774, at the age of 66.

Chapter 5:
The First American

Franklin and the American Revolution

Franklin proposed a national congress in 1754, at a congregation of colonial representatives in Albany, New York. His goal was to unite the colonies into a single entity, with the ultimate aim to function as an autonomous state. His plan was rejected, but parts of it were later used in the Articles of Confederation, the first federal governing documents produced by the United States in 1781, before the Constitution was ratified and adopted.

Like most of the colonists, Franklin considered himself a loyal Englishman early in his career overseas. He had an extraordinary fondness for the country, which had fine thinkers, theater, witty conversation— things in short supply in America. During his time abroad, Franklin did his best to avert the Revolution. He used his connections in England to help improve English opinions of Americans. He wrote articles and satirical pieces, and used these to demonstrate to his many English friends that Americans were not the provincial rubes many considered them to be. He tried extremely hard to improve the relationship between the colonies and England, and constantly strove to enlighten the ruling class of England about the conditions and sentiment in the colonies.

Franklin returned to London right when tensions between Great Britain and the American colonies were at an all-time high. Parliament's passage of the Stamp Act in 1765 had imposed a highly unpopular tax on all printed materials used for commercial or legal purposes in the colonies. Franklin's passionate denunciation of the tax before Parliament contributed significantly to the repeal of the

Stamp Act in 1766, and is perhaps the greatest example of his rhetorical prowess in terms of direct results.

This made Franklin extremely popular in the colonies, and because of this, he became the primary voice in support of colonial interests in England. He wrote popular essays on behalf of the colonies, including his 1768 pamphlet *Causes of the American Discontents before 1768*. He became the representative for colonies beyond Pennsylvania, and soon spoke for Georgia, New Jersey, and Massachusetts. But his support for England was short-lived, and he soon began to believe that America should become its own sovereign nation, echoing his previous plan to unite the colonies in 1754. Despite his friendliness with a great many among the English gentry, Franklin grew sickened by the level of political and royal corruption he noticed.

Eventually, when new taxes were issued for the colonies, Franklin had had enough. He began to earnestly support the American independence movement.

What had truly spoiled his view of English rule was not that taxes had been issued, but that English citizens residing in Britain were not subjected to the same taxes. As most colonists, including Franklin, considered themselves to be English citizens, they viewed this unequal taxation as fundamentally unjust and morally bankrupt. The word "tyranny" soon spread throughout the colonies, and Franklin did his level best to support efforts to undermine English rule.

Franklin continued to fan the flames of discontent and revolution during the Hutchinson Letters Affair. In 1773, the English-appointed governor of Massachusetts was a man named Thomas Hutchinson. He feigned support for the people of Massachusetts as they denounced many of the policies of England, but he privately supported and worked closely with King George III. Somehow, Franklin procured private correspondence from the governor, in which Hutchinson called for the restriction of the rights of colonists in America. He sent the letters to America, where much of the population was outraged once they were reprinted in Boston newspapers. After leaking the letters, Franklin was called to Whitehall, the English Foreign Ministry, where he was condemned in public and removed from his post as deputy postmaster general. Franklin remained in England for several years, but his efforts to reconcile the conflicting claims between Parliament and the colonies were unsuccessful. He returned to America in 1775 devoted to the patriot cause.

Upon his return, Franklin began working actively for Independence. He assumed that his son William, then the Royal governor of New Jersey, would agree with his views and follow suit. William did not share his father's view, however, and remained loyal to Britain. This caused a rift between them that never healed. The New Jersey militia stripped William Franklin of his post as New Jersey's royal governor and imprisoned him, but his father chose not to intercede on his behalf this time.

Franklin returned to Philadelphia in May of 1775, shortly after the Revolutionary War had begun, and was elected to serve as a delegate to the Second Continental Congress, America's governing body at the time. He was also appointed the first postmaster general for the colonies during this period. In 1776, he was appointed commissioner to Canada and worked on a committee of five men who worked to draft the Declaration of Independence. In this document, all thirteen American colonies declared to the world their freedom from British rule and tyranny. Though much of the actual writing and verbiage was Thomas Jefferson's, many conceptual contributions were Franklin's.

In 1776, Franklin signed the Declaration along with fifty-five other patriots, then traveled to France to serve as an ambassador to the Court of Louis XVI. Franklin was charged with gaining French support against the British in order to aid the war effort. In February of 1778, France signed a military alliance with America, and went on to provide soldiers, supplies, and money to the colonies. They had their own motivations, but their recognition of America as its own entity helped legitimize the efforts of the fledgling nation.

Statesman and Diplomat

Franklin's years in Paris serving as what was basically the first ambassador to France, and particularly his romantic life, continues to be a topic of discussion today. When his wife, Deborah, passed away, Franklin pursued many women during his nine years of service, and even proposed to Madame Helvetius, a widow, when he was seventy-four, though she turned him down.

Franklin was immensely popular in France. His intellect and wit, along with the respect he gained from the scientific community combined with his political reputation made him a respected figure. The novelty of the newly formed American nation also helped him gain social status. Even King Louis XVI respected the man, and he was allowed entry into the most exclusive social circles. Eventually, his diplomatic acumen led him to become a key player in ending the American Revolution, culminating in the Treaty of Paris in 1783, which officially ended hostilities between England and America. Without his support and advocacy, that treaty may have never been signed.

Franklin was eventually replaced as French ambassador by Thomas Jefferson, who paid tribute to his long list of accomplishments and respected reputation, saying, "I succeed him; no one can replace him."

Final Years

Two years after the peace treaty in 1783, Congress finally permitted Franklin to return home. He arrived in 1785, by then in his late seventies, though he did not stop to rest. Immediately upon his return, he was elected President of the Council of Pennsylvania, and was subsequently reelected, even though he protested vehemently.

He was elected in to serve as Pennsylvania's delegate to the Constitutional Convention of 1787, during which the Constitution of the United States was drafted and framed. Franklin was the oldest delegate, at the age of eighty-one. At the convention, Franklin did not often speak, but when he did, it was always to the point. Many of his suggestions and the points that he raised made it into the final draft, and the Constitution would not be the same without his input. In September of 1787, at the end of the Convention, Franklin urged his fellow delegates to support and join him in signing the heavily-debated document. He happily affixed his signature to it, just as he had done for other monumentally important American documents, such as the Declaration of Independence and the Treaty of Paris. The United States Constitution was ratified by the required nine states in June of 1788, and George Washington was inaugurated as America's first president in April of 1789.

Arguably the most important proposal by Franklin to the Constitution was the Great Compromise. After the failure of the Articles of Confederation, the delegation at the convention was split into Federalist and Anti-federalist supporters. A populist movement had grown due to the states' many failures, but anti-federalist supporters of state sovereignty argued that the state governments deserved a say in the governance of the nation as a whole. Initially, Franklin supported the idea that proportional representation was the fairest way to populate Congressional delegates. However, he was eventually swayed by smaller states with fewer people, who believed that they deserved their own vote. To accommodate both groups, Franklin proposed the Great Compromise, which created a bicameral Congress. One house, the House of Representatives, would have 435 congressmen, and would be assigned based on population. The second, the Senate, would provide two senators for each state, all with an equal vote.

As originally designed, senators were not elected, but actually appointed by each state's legislature. This ensured that the state governments would all have their say in the governance of the nation, a key component of the compromise between the federalists and anti-federalists. In 1911, however, Congress passed the 17th Amendment, which changed the process to popular election rather than appointment. This ran counter to Franklin's original intent, which was to provide representation for state *governments* rather than the state's *population*. The House was supposed to represent the people, while the Senate represented the states.

After the convention, Franklin helped found the Society for Political Inquiries, an organization dedicated to improving knowledge of government. In his later years, he also became more outspoken in his opposition to slavery. He served as president of the Pennsylvania Society for Promoting the Abolition of Slavery, writing many tracts supporting abolition. One of Franklin's last public acts was writing an anti-slavery treatise in 1789, in which he petitioned the United States Congress to abolish slavery and the slave trade.

Benjamin Franklin's work was done. At the age of eighty-two, he finally retired from public service. He suffered great physical pain, yet maintained a positive outlook. During this time he wrote many letters, about a hundred of which have been preserved. These letters demonstrate no retrospection or regrets. Throughout his life, Franklin always looked forward, and he constantly sought the next phase of progress and improvement for himself and those who surrounded him. In his final years, Franklin continued work on his autobiography, in which Franklin reflected on his remarkable and highly influential life and career.

Chapter 6:

A Man of Science

1700s Science and Mechanical Ingenuity

Franklin was not just a man of politics and public service, but was renowned as a man of science. He first demonstrated his mechanical ingenuity when he worked as a printer. Printing was tedious and difficult work, and a printer had to be something of a mechanic as well as a writer and a typesetter. While he worked at this trade, Franklin invented new methods of casting type and making ink.

Franklin studied many different branches of science, and had greatly varied scientific interests. He studied smoky chimneys and proposed fire prevention practices, studied the effects of oil upon ruffled water, advocated for ventilation during the days when windows were closed tightly at night, and at all times for those who were ill. He investigated new fertilizers to improve agricultural practices, attributed the "dry bellyache" to lead poisoning, and more. Franklin's scientific observations demonstrate his clear foresight regarding some of the great developments of the nineteenth century.

Franklin's discoveries and inventions also included social innovations, such as the concept of "paying it forward." His many innovations and scientific inquiry were mostly driven by an altruistic motive. He never patented his inventions, but rather offered them freely, hoping that society would benefit, and always aimed to increase efficiency and promote human improvement. On the topic, he once wrote, "As we enjoy great advantages from the inventions of others, we should be glad of an opportunity to serve others by any invention of ours; and this we should do freely and generously."

Scientist and Inventor

Franklin proved himself to be a savvy businessman, and in the 1730's and 1740's, his printing business thrived. He grew and expanded it, and opened franchises and partnerships in many other cities. By 1748, he was successful enough that he was able to retire, and through a lucrative business arrangement, he was able to maintain a life of public service and, just as important to him, scientific inquiry.

Because he did not patent his inventions, dating his innovations is difficult, and any dates given are approximate, except where indicated.

In the 1740s and 50s, he conducted several experiments that contributed to the understanding of electricity. He invented the lightning rod, which protected buildings from fires caused by lightning. In the early 1750s, he conducted his famous kite experiment, which proved that lightning is comprised of electricity. His observations brought Franklin international fame.

Franklin was also an impressive inventor. Among his many creations and inventions are the Franklin stove, which provided more heat while using less fuel than other stoves, enabling homes to be heated more efficiently, bifocal spectacles, which allow for distance and reading use, swimming flippers, and the flexible urinary catheter. In the early 1760s, Franklin improved a musical instrument called the armonica (which is made of glass, and is not to be confused with the metal harmonica). Composers such as Ludwig Beethoven and Wolfgang Mozart wrote music for Franklin's armonica. However, by the early part of the 19th century, the once-popular instrument largely fell out of use.

Lightning Rods

The lightning rod was a direct result of Franklin's experiments with electricity. During these experiments, he realized that conductors that had pointed ends rather than smooth ones discharged their current silently and directionally, and that the distance of the discharge was significantly greater. He understood the potential of this discovery, and theorized that he could develop this knowledge into an apparatus that would protect buildings from lightning strikes. He envisioned "upright Rods of Iron, made sharp as a needle and gilt to prevent rusting, and from the foot of those rods a wire down the outside of the building into the ground. Would not these pointed rods probably draw the electrical fire silently out of a cloud before it came nigh enough to strike, and thereby secure us from that most sudden and terrible mischief!"

After he experimented with different designs on his own house, he installed lightning rods on the Academy of Philadelphia, which he had founded, and the Pennsylvania State House in 1752, and they are still used on buildings today.

The Franklin Stove

As Franklin's understanding of science grew, he studied the transfer of heat. After various experiments, he closely evaluated the designs of the stoves that were typically used at the time, and realized that they were inefficient. The flues of these stoves channeled far too much of the heat upward, away from the areas where the heat was actually desired. Using his discoveries, Franklin redesigned these stoves, basing the new blueprints on his observations of heat exchange.

His observations were that hot gasses typically rose to the top of the flue and exchanged heat with colder air from the room. From there, the cold air warmed, and thus the room was heated. The Franklin Stove, or Pennsylvania Stove, was designed with these principles in mind, and provided a far more efficient use of fuel sources than traditional heating apparatus. It was quickly made available for purchase and use in homes, and homeowners were able to heat their houses with far less fuel.

Bifocal Spectacles

Franklin wore spectacles for the majority of his life, but he found his spectacles extremely limiting, however, because a lens that was used for reading blurred his vision when he looked up at something in the distance. In Franklin's trade as a printer, this was nothing but distracting and potentially infuriating.

Franklin found a way around the problem by developing split-lens bifocal spectacles. Each

lens was affixed with two focusing distances—
one for reading, and one for distance. Looking
through the bottom part of the lens provided
clearer vision for reading, while looking
through the upper portion of the lens offered
clearer vision at a greater distance.

Areas of Study and Exploration

Demographics, or the study of population
growth and distribution, was a new science
during Franklin's time, and he provided a
major influence on it. During the 1730s and
1740s, Franklin tracked population growth,
and found that the American population was
growing faster than anywhere else on the
planet. He calculated that America's
population was doubling approximately every
twenty years, and within one hundred years
would surpass England's population. In 1751,

he drafted *Observations Concerning the Increase of Mankind*, which was printed anonymously in Boston four years later, then quickly reprinted in England, where it influenced the economists Adam Smith and Thomas Malthus. This work remains one of the leading works of eighteenth-century Anglo-American demography. Franklin's piece scared English citizens, who feared that a rapidly expanding colonial population surpassing their own would result in revolution. To prevent this, ironically, they began to impose restrictions upon the colonial economy, including tax policies, many of which were among the causes of the American Revolution.

Wave Theory of Light

Christiaan Huygens proposed the wave theory of light in 1678, which states that light was comprised of vibrating waves. The vast majority of scientists disregarded this theory, and instead supported Newton's particle theory of light, or the corpuscular theory.

Franklin, however, disagreed with these scientists, and was a strong supporter of Huygens's theory. In 1803, Thomas Young conducted the widely documented slit experiment, which rocked the scientific community. It essentially confirmed Huygens's theory that light functions as a wave.

This slit experiment occurred after Franklin's death, but confirms and demonstrates his intelligence and willingness to ignore popular opinion and pressure from his contemporaries.

Meteorology

According to legend, a lunar eclipse that Franklin dearly wanted to witness on October

21st, 1743, was blocked by a storm. Franklin, incensed that he had missed the opportunity, studied the storm, and realized that it had moved into his area from the southwest— according to letters from his brother, it hadn't reached Boston, which was to the northeast of Benjamin, until *after* the eclipse. However, the prevailing winds traveled from the northeast. This led to the revelation that weather systems did *not* travel exclusively by the prevailing winds, which had a significant impact on meteorology for years to come.

Oceanography

In his later years, Franklin accumulated all of his oceanographic findings into a work titled *Maritime Observations*, which was published by the Philosophical Society in 1786. The book detailed new concepts for sea anchors, compartments that were watertight, lightning rods that could be placed onboard ships, new hulls for catamarans, and a soup bowl with improvements that allowed it to remain steady during poor weather.

Atlantic Ocean Currents

During his stay in England, in 1768, the Colonial Board of Customs issued a complaint. They wanted to know the reason British mail ships took several weeks longer to reach New York than it did for merchant vessels to reach Newport, Rhode Island. The problem was particularly perplexing, as the merchant vessels had to travel a complex route to leave from London while the mail ships left from more favorable conditions in Cornwall.

Timothy Folger, Franklin's cousin and a whaler out of Nantucket, answered Benjamin's question. He explained that merchant captains understood that there was an extremely strong current in the middle of the ocean, which pushed from west to east. These ships took measures to travel around this current, while the mail vessels went straight through it, fighting it the whole way. As it traveled at about three miles per hour, this slowed down the mail ships significantly, which resulted in a several week delay.

Franklin, Folger, and a variety of other ship captains made significant strides to chart this current in an effort to improve mail carriage. He named it the Gulf Stream, which remains its term to this day.

Franklin published his findings in 1770, but the English disregarded it entirely. In 1778, it was republished in France, and made its way to the United States in 1786. The original chart, which had been completely ignored, was assumed lost, but Phil Richards, an oceanographer, found it in Paris in 1980, and the story was printed on the front page of the *New York Times.*

It was years before British sailors accepted Franklin's proposals, but once they did, their travel time was cut by two weeks.

Refrigeration and Cooling

On a particularly warm day, Franklin realized that he was far more comfortable in a wet shirt than a dry one, especially when a breeze came through. He had unknowingly stumbled upon one of the key principles of refrigeration. Franklin sought to explain *why* this was the case. In 1758, while he was in Cambridge, Franklin and John Hadley, another scientist, took a standard mercury thermometer, and moistened its end with ether. They then used a bellows to evaporate the liquid, and repeated the process. Every time they evaporated the ether, the temperature on the thermometer dropped, and eventually fell to seven degrees Fahrenheit. However, a second thermometer in the room showed that the temperature elsewhere had remained a steady sixty-five degrees Fahrenheit.

Franklin did not have the scientific knowledge that is accessible today, and therefore could not explain the molecular heat transfer that was taking place, but he did realize that evaporation resulted in cooling, which was an important stride in the industry of refrigeration.

Effect of Temperature on Electrical Conductivity

Franklin conducted a wide range of experiments on ice concerning conductivity. He realized that the loss of heat in a conductor led to a corresponding reduction in conductivity. This was later codified by other scientists, who established the law of liquefaction of electrolytes, but Franklin himself laid the groundwork, and may have understood it before anyone else did. In his own words, he discovered that "A certain quantity of heat will make some bodies good conductors that will not otherwise conduct," and "water, though naturally a good conductor, will not conduct well when frozen into ice."

Decision-making

Franklin was well-known for his logic and organization skills. In a 1772 letter to his friend Joseph Priestly, he demonstrated what may actually be the very first description of a Pro and Con list, a widely used method to make informed and logical decisions.

"My Way is, to divide half a Sheet of Paper by a Line into two Columns, writing over the one Pro, and over the other Con. Then during three or four Days Consideration I put down under the different Heads short Hints of the different Motives that at different Times occur to me for or against the Measure. When I have thus got them all together in one View, I endeavor to estimate their respective Weights; and where I find two, one on each side, that seem equal, I strike them both out: If I find a Reason pro equal to some two Reasons con, I strike out the three. If I judge some two Reasons con equal to some three Reasons pro, I strike out the five; and thus proceeding I find at length where the Balance lies; and if after a Day or two of farther Consideration nothing new that is of Importance occurs on either side, I come to a Determination accordingly."

Chess

Franklin was also the first chess player in the American colonies that is known by name, and it has been verified that he had played by 1733. An extremely avid player, he wrote an essay titled *The Morals of Chess*, in which he praises the game, and details appropriate behavior when playing it. The essay was published in *Columbian Magazine* in 1786, and is only the second American written piece concerning chess. It has been reprinted and translated countless times since its publication.

During his time in England, Franklin played chess far more frequently, and was able to challenge more experienced opponents, because the game had been established there for quite some time. As a result of the fiercer opposition, Franklin grew more skilled at chess, and his victory rate increased. He used chess to socialize and make contacts with various Englishmen, particularly in the Old Slaughter's Coffee house, which he frequented. The connections he forged during these games served him well for the rest of his life. While in Paris, during his service as an ambassador, Franklin was a frequent customer of the Café de la Régence. France's strongest players regularly gathered there in order to play serious games. No records of Franklin's games and conquests have survived, however, so measuring his skill against modern players is not possible.

Franklin was posthumously inducted into the United States Chess Hall of Fame in 1999. The Franklin Mercantile Chess Club in Philadelphia, the second oldest chess club in the U.S., is named for him.

Musical Interests

Aside from scientific pursuits, Franklin was an accomplished musician, and played the violin, harp, and guitar. He composed his own music as well, including an early classical style string quarter piece, which can still be heard today.

However, his inventive nature also combined with his love for music. He invented a new and radically improved glass armonica. Earlier versions of the instrument required that the player rotate their fingers along the edges of the glasses, which made it difficult and tiring to play. Franklin developed a shaft, around which the glasses rotated, while the player held their fingers steady. Eventually, his new design caught on, and it reached Europe, where Beethoven, Mozart, and other composers wrote pieces for it.

Benjamin Franklin and Electricity

Franklin's greatest fame as a scientist came as a result of his experiments and discoveries in electricity. During a visit to his home town of Boston in 1746, the always curious Franklin attended a science show, where he watched some electrical experiments, and he at once became deeply interested. At the show, he saw Dr. Archibald Spencer, a Scottish scientist, demonstrate a variety of scientific concepts and phenomena.

The parts of the demonstration that included electricity excited Franklin more than any of the others, particularly the effects of static electricity. Franklin immediately wanted to learn more about it. Franklin eventually came to believe that Dr. Spencer did not truly understand it, but this time in history, *no one* understood electricity, and it was more a subject of speculation and entertainment than an area of legitimate scientific study.

Franklin soon acquired the most advanced electrical apparatus available, which was crude by today's standards, from his London friend Peter Collinson. He also purchased a variety of equipment in Boston, including a lengthy tube that he could use to efficiently and quickly generate static electricity. Within a short time, the majority of Franklin's spare time was spent studying electricity. In a letter to Collinson, he wrote, "For my own part, I never was before engaged in any study that so engrossed my attention and my time as this has lately done."

Shaping Understanding of Electricity

Franklin's letters to Collinson detail his first forays into electrical experimentation. With a small group of friends, he conducted a demonstration of pointed lightning rods and the ways in which they were able to draw redirect current. This experiment led him to conclude that friction did not cause electricity, but that it was actually diffused through most substances, and that equilibrium was always restored.

He also mentions a variety of tricks and practical jokes that he and his friends often played on their neighbors. Using electricity, they ignited alcohol, relit candles that had been extinguished, mimicked lightning strikes and flashes of light, and caused a fake spider to move mysteriously, seemingly on its own.

Franklin also developed a new kind of electrical battery, a term that he coined. It referred to something very different than modern batteries, however. His battery was a series of capacitors, Leyden jars, which were wired into a series. This resulted in a much greater storage capacity than previous iterations were able to match. Because of this, Franklin was able to produce much larger discharges than the vast majority of other experimenters.

His experiments included a wide range of practical (and less practical, but no less interesting) applications. He continued to experiment with Leyden jars, and eventually improved upon their design. He cooked a fowl he had hunted by roasting it on a spit that rotated with electricity. He used water to conduct enough current to ignite a pool of alcohol, and used electricity to set off a small charge of gunpowder. He also charged glasses of wine with electricity, which delivered a shock to the drinker when they took a sip, which did not prove much, but delighted Franklin's boyish nature.

Perhaps most importantly, he developed the theory of positive and negative electricity.
Franklin's observations soon began to shape the world's understanding of electricity and the language used to talk about it— language that is still used today. For example, Franklin asserted that an "electrical fluid" exists that could flow from one point to another. To describe this process, he coined the terms "positive" and "negative" to outline the differences between the two points after the electrical fluid had flowed. This was among the first observations of what would later be revealed to be electrons.

Franklin believed that this "fluid," when present in excess amounts, produced a positive charge, and that smaller amounts of this fluid produced a negative charge. He was also the first person to realize that electrical charges could never actually be *created*, but could only be collected, or gathered into an area. This was later codified as the Law of Conservation of Electrical Charge.

In 1750, Franklin published a proposal for an experiment to prove that lightning is electricity by flying a kite in a lightning storm. In 1751, Franklin published a book called *Experiments and Observations on Electricity*, a collection of his results. The book was widely read in Europe, and demonstrated that America was a global leader in understanding electricity.

On May 10th, 1752, Thomas-François Dalibard, a French scientist, conducted the experiment Franklin mentioned, only he used a forty-foot iron rod instead of a kite. The experiment was a success, and he was able to extract electrical sparks from a cloud.

Sources vary, but on June 15th of that year, it appears that Franklin conducted his well-known kite and key experiment in Philadelphia, also successfully extracting sparks from a cloud. The results were later written by Joseph Priestly, and Franklin was credited in 1767.

The dangers of the experiment were not lost on Franklin. He made sure that he was insulated, and that he stood outside of a conducting path to avoid electrocution. Despite this, several attempts to replicate his experiment, including some conducted by notable professors and scientists, resulted in electrocution and death.

The common portrayal of Franklin's experiment— in which he fixed a key to a kite, flew it into a storm cloud, and waited for lightning to strike it— is certainly incorrect. Well aware of the danger, Franklin used the kite to collect charges in the form of sparks from a storm cloud, and thereby proved that lightning was comprised of electricity.

To emphasize the dangers and to outline the proper procedure to replicate his results, Franklin wrote a letter to English scientists on October 19th of that year:

"When rain has wet the kite twine so that it can conduct the electric fire freely, you will find it streams out plentifully from the key at the approach of your knuckle, and with this key a phial, or Leyden jar, may be charged: and from electric fire thus obtained spirits may be kindled, and all other electric experiments [may be] performed which are usually done by the help of a rubber glass globe or tube; and therefore the sameness of the electrical matter with that of lightening completely demonstrated."

Franklin's experiment firmly established electrical study as a legitimate discipline and scientific focus. Until this point, the concept of electricity was mostly seen as entertainment or was considered merely speculative, the equivalent of fringe science today. However, Franklin's experiment proved that electricity was found in nature, and functioned as a powerful and observable force in the environment. After this experiment, electricity was never considered to be a simple plaything, something used by showmen for entertainment.

In 1753, at age 47, Franklin's transformative experiments were recognized. Correspondence between him and Collinson was originally brought to the Royal Society, of which Collinson was a member, but they were virtually unnoticed. Collinson instead brought them together and had them read the conclusions. He published the results, and they gained wide attention and acclaim. Once they were translated into French, they were mostly recognized and accepted by the scientific community. In 1753, Franklin was awarded the Copley Medal, which was comparable to the modern Nobel Prize, and he was later invited to become a Fellow of the Royal Society of Britain, one of a handful of Americans to do so at the time.

Chapter 7:
Death and Legacy

Dead at 84 Years Old

In 1790, shortly after he petitioned to Congress to abolish slavery, Franklin died at the age of eighty-four in Philadelphia at the home of his daughter, Sarah. Franklin suffered from gout, and had complained of ailments for some time, including persistent effects from a bout of pleurisy, an inflammation of the lungs, in his younger years. Over twenty thousand people attended his funeral. He was laid to rest in Christ Church Burial Ground.

Franklin completed a final codicil to his will just over a year and a half before his death. He bequeathed most of his estate to Sarah, and left very little to his son William. Benjamin had never quite overcome his son's opposition to American independence, and their relationship suffered as a result. In his will, he left sums of money to Boston and Philadelphia. These funds were later used to establish a trade school and a science museum, and funded scholarships and other community projects.

In his will, Franklin was characteristically modest; he described himself simply as a printer, ambassador to France, and resident of Pennsylvania. He certainly could have noted that he had also been a famous and well-respected scientist, an inventor, a successful author and publisher, a philanthropist, a statesman, and a draftsman of both the Declaration and Independence and the United States Constitution, but he left those things out, preferring to see himself in simpler terms.

Franklin provided his own epitaph, which he wrote when he was just twenty-two:

"The body of B. Franklin, Printer (Like the Cover of an Old Book Its Contents torn Out And Stript of its Lettering and Gilding) Lies

Here, and Food for Worms. But the Work shall not be Lost; For it will (as he Believ'd) Appear once More In a New and More Elegant Edition Revised and Corrected By the Author." In the end, however, the stone on the grave he shared with his wife in the cemetery of Philadelphia's Christ Church reads simply, "Benjamin and Deborah Franklin 1790."

Bequest

Franklin bequeathed £1,000 each to the cities of Boston and Philadelphia. He mandated that these funds be placed in a trust to gather interest for 200 years. The trust was opened in 1785 when French mathematician Charles-Joseph Mathon de la Cour, a great admirer of Franklin, wrote a friendly parody of Franklin's *Poor Richard's Almanac* called *Fortunate Richard*. In *Fortunate Richard*, the main character left equal sums of money to each collect interest over various lengths of time (the first was held for one century, the second for two centuries, and so on). The vast amount of money that resulted from the compounded interest was mandated to be spent on outrageously complex community projects.

Franklin, who was seventy-nine years old at the time, wrote to the author. He thanked him for the inspiration and told him that he planned to leave one thousand pounds to Boston and one thousand pounds to Philadelphia in an attempt to recreate the fiction.

Franklin was as good as his word, and issued the bequest. For the first 100 years, the money was to be placed in a trust and only used to provide loans to local tradesmen. After that, some portion could then be spent, but the rest was required to remain off limits for another 100 years, at which point each city could use it as they saw fit.

By 1990, the Philadelphia trust had accumulated more than $2,000,000. Between 1940 and 1990, the money was used primarily for mortgage loans. When the trust came due, Philadelphia decided to spend the money on scholarships for local high school students. Franklin's Boston trust fund had similarly grown to nearly $5,000,000 during that same time. When the trust came due in Boston, a portion was allocated to help establish a trade school that became the Franklin Institute of Boston, and the remainder of the fund was later dedicated to supporting this institute.

Remembered and Memorialized

The image of Benjamin Franklin that has prevailed through history, along his likeness shown on the $100 bill, is something of a caricature: a bald man in a frock coat holding a kite string with a key attached. But the scope of things to which Franklin dedicated and applied himself was so broad that limiting his familiar likeness to only one of his many endeavors does his memory a disservice.

Franklin was a true Renaissance Man. Among many interests and accomplishments, Franklin founded universities and libraries, the United States Post Office, shaped the foreign policy of the United States, drafted and signed the Declaration of Independence, and published newspapers and composed many types of literature. Franklin warmed Americans with the Franklin stove, pioneered scientific advances, helped Americans see with bifocal lenses, and advanced the study of electricity by decades.

What makes this truly remarkable is that all of this came from the mind of a man who never finished more than two years of formal education, but continued to shape his own life through constant reading and experience, a strong moral compass, and an unflagging commitment to civic duty. Franklin was a true learner, a true polymath, and a true entrepreneur.

Franklin's fascinatingly diverse life, coupled with his reputation as a Founding Father, provided ample cause for Franklin to be honored and memorialized in many ways, from coins to the $100 bill, from names of warships to the names of many towns, counties, educational institutions, businesses, and corporations, and now more than two centuries after his death, countless other items, locations, and cultural references.

A wide variety of landmarks in and around Philadelphia are named after him, as it is the town in which he spent most of his life. Listing every individual place and institution that bears his name would take far too long. There are currently 151 entities named in his honor.

There is also the Benjamin Franklin Medal, a science and engineering award, which reflects and celebrates Franklin's interests in science and engineering. It is still one of the highest honors in scientific fields, and its winners include Alexander Graham Bell, Marie and Pierre Curie, Albert Einstein, and Stephen Hawking.

Recreational activities also celebrate Franklin's interests and influence. The Franklin Mercantile Chess Club in Philadelphia, the second oldest chess club in the U.S., is named in Franklin's honor, for example, as he was the first American chess writer.

Epilogue

The United States would not be the same country it is today if it was not for Benjamin Franklin. Indeed, the *world* would not be the same without his presence. His influence on our culture, our political system, and our understanding of science and the natural world can be neither understated nor underestimated. His list of contributions to various areas of study are so wide and varied that they continue to impress today.

The Great Compromise, which established the bicameral Congress, may be his most enduring contribution to history. Without it, the very nature of American society and politics would be dramatically different.

Perhaps equally important was his scientific work, however, which advanced the study of electricity by decades, and paved the way for the likes of Edison and Tesla to provide a huge amount of amenities and conveniences that are considered necessary for daily life.

Or maybe it was his philosophy that was most important— *Poor Richard's Almanac* still provides an enormous amount of quotes that are used today, and his Thirteen Virtues are still used in self-help books read around the globe.

But the reality is that Franklin did not make anyone choose what his most important leap forward was; he simply provided the advancement, and asked for little in return. His externally-focused and civic-minded nature drove him to perform incredible feats of statesmanship, diplomacy, ingenuity, and innovation. He did not seek material rewards for his work, but rather did the work because he felt it was necessary, because he believed it would better society, and because he enjoyed the act of helping others.

Perhaps Franklin's greatest legacy is his generous spirit. Maybe the image of a man with bifocals is not the one that should spring to mind when his name is mentioned. Instead, maybe we should recall a man who once walked down the street with everything he owned on his back and in his hands, and gave what little he had left to a child and her mother for no other reason than they were hungry.

In Franklin's own words as written in *Poor Richard's Almanac,* "To be humble to superiors is duty, to equals courtesy, to inferiors nobleness."

Franklin lived up to those words his entire life, and his humility and generosity make him all the more fascinating, enduring, and respected.

Sources

Andrews, Evan. "11 Surprising Facts About Benjamin Franklin." History.com. A&E Television Networks, 2016. Web. 2 Feb. 2016.

"Benjamin Franklin Biography." Bio.com. Ed. Biography.com Editors. A&E Networks Television, 2016. Web. 2 Feb. 2016.

"Benjamin Franklin." Famous Scientists. famousscientists,org. 1 Jul. 2014. Web. 4 Feb. 2016.

"Benjamin Franklin His Autobiography 1706-1757." Journal of Occurrences in My Voyage to Philadelphia. Ed. George M. Welling. University of Groningen, 2012. Web. 5 Feb. 2016.

"Benjamin Franklin His Autobiography 1706-1757." A Short Biography. Ed. George M. Welling. University of Groningen, 2012. Web. 3 Feb. 2016.

Bortman, Eli. "Franklin, Benjamin." Encyclopedia of American Studies. Ed. Simon Bronner. : Johns Hopkins University Press, 2014.Credo Reference. Web. 11 Feb. 2016.

Franklin, Benjamin. The Autobiography of Benjamin Franklin. New York: Dover Publications, 1996. Print.

The Franklin Institute. "Benjamin Franklin FAQ." Benjamin Franklin FAQ. The Franklin Institute, 2015. Web. 3 Feb. 2016.

History.com Staff. "Benjamin Franklin." History.com. A&E Television Networks, 2009. Web. 2 Feb. 2016.

Hornberger, Theodore, and Gordon S. Wood. "Benjamin Franklin | American Author, Scientist, and Statesman." Encyclopedia Britannica Online. Encyclopedia Britannica, 2016. Web. 7 Feb. 2016.

"Josiah Franklin." Wikipedia. Wikimedia Foundation, 2015. Web. 1 Feb. 2016.

"Mary Morrill." Wikipedia. Wikimedia Foundation, 2015. Web. 1 Feb. 2016.

"Peter Foulger." Wikipedia. Wikimedia Foundation, 2015. Web. 1 Feb. 2016.

Pettinger, Tejvan. "Benjamin Franklin Biography •." Biography Online. Tejvan Pettinger, 5 Feb. 2010. Web. 2 Feb. 2016.

"Quick Biography of Benjamin Franklin." Ushistory.org. Independence Hall Association, 2014. Web. 1 Feb. 2016.

Sparks, Jared. "Life of Benjamin Franklin (by Jared Sparks): Index Page." Ushistory.org. Independence Hall Association, 2014. Web. 2 Feb. 2016.

Stewart, Greg. "Illustrious Brother Ben Franklin and Freemasonry." Freemason Information. Freemason Information, 17 Jan. 2015. Web. 9 Feb. 2016.

"The Story of Benjamin Franklin: Birth & Early Childhood." About.com Inventors. About.com, 2016. Web. 2 Feb. 2016.

Thompson, Holland. "Benjamin Franklin and His Times." The Age of Invention: A Chronicle of Mechanical Conquest. Vol. 37. New Haven: Yale UP, 1921. 1-31. Chronicles of America. The Age of Invention: A Chronicle of Mechanical Conquest. Yale University Press, 20 June 2014. Web. 4 Feb. 2016.

"Timeline (1657-1719) - The Benjamin Franklin Tercentenary." Timeline (1657-1719) - The Benjamin Franklin Tercentenary. The

Benjamin Franklin Tercentenary, 2008. Web. 2 Feb. 2016.

University of Pennsylvania. "University of Pennsylvania." Penn's Heritage. The University of Pennsylvania, 2016. Web. 10 Feb. 2016.

USHistory.org. "Benjamin Franklin." Ushistory.org. Independence Hall Association, 2014. Web. 5 Feb. 2016.

Made in the USA
Lexington, KY
02 November 2016